Gai's Go-Away-Come-Back Garden

Sandy Baker

Illustrated by
Jack Wiens

Black Garnet Press
Santa Rosa, CA

Gai's Go-Away-Come-Back Garden

To all who've thrilled to the sight of fireflies —Sandy

In memory of Hugh Jones who loved growing food for his family —Jack

ISBN 978-0-9911790-3-9

Designed by Rita Ter Sarkissoff • www.springhillbooks.com • Printed in USA

Also by Sandy Baker

- *Three Sisters Garden, 2014*
- *Howie's Hungabird Dilemma, 2014*
- *Color My Garden (English and Spanish versions) 2013*
- *The Dead Butterflies Diary, 2013*
- *Zack's Zany Zucchiniland, 2012*
- *Mrs. Feeny and the Grubby Garden Gang, 2011*
- *The Iehran Triangle (with Tom Reed), 2012*
- Editor, *The Reagan Enigma: 1964-1980*, by Thomas C. Reed, 2014

See more of the author's eclectic stuff at www.sandybakerwriter.com

"Go away," snarled Gai. "I don't need no darn babysitter. I'm not a baby. Mom and Dad're gone for two weeks? You gotta be kidding."

"Look, Gai, you and I are gonna hang out," said Gina. "Your dad has business, and your mom wanted to travel with him. We'll have a good time together."

"Yeah? Like doin' what?" Gai sneered.

"Well, for starters, I'd like to see your garden. Your mom said I should check it out while the flowers are blooming."

"Oh, boy, big deal. Besides, it's not MY garden. It's my mom's and she complains I weed the wrong things and get in her way."

"Not to worry, gardens are for kids, too," laughed Gina. "C'mon."

"Oh-KAY . . . It's so stupid how she mixes flowers and vegetables all in together. She says sometimes that helps keep bad bugs away."

"It's mostly true but look at these little bite marks, Gai. Quick, do you have a magnifying glass? And bring out a plastic container with a lid, okay?"

Gai and Gina took turns looking at the holes in the tomato and marigold foliage.

"Look here, the tomatoes have a major problem."

"Wow, a fat creepy thing with a horn! An ugly monster from another planet!"

"Guess what it's called— a tomato hornworm," said Gina. "Let's find more and put them in the container."

"Do they bite?"

"No, but they might wiggle or curl up. Just pick 'em off as fast as you can. See how they're the same color as the tomato leaves— that's their camouflage. We'll dump 'em in the garbage later."

"Really? Maybe I can share 'em in Show an' Tell?"

"These'll be way dead. Catch more right before school begins," Gina laughed.

"I want to show you something else," she said. "See this shiny stuff on the stepping stones? Night visitors. We'll look after dinner."

Later, Gina and Gai spotted tiny flashes dotting the dark indigo sky.

"Can I text Mom and Dad on your cell phone?" Gai asked.

"Gonna catch lightning bugs," he tapped and waited.

"Have fun, Son. Good sleep. Hugs. Mom & Dad," they texted back.

"Bring out two flashlights, okay? I have a surprise for you."

Gai carried out the flashlights, hammer, a jar, and nail in a plastic bag. After Gina punched some holes in the lid, he ran back and forth catching the fireflies.

"Hey, buddy, we're going to do something special now."

"Bring the bag and flashlights and let's go. We're detectives looking for clues. Look there," said Gina. "See that silvery, slimy trail I showed you before? We'll follow it with the light. See . . . see . . . look at that."

⭐ 11

"What IS that? Oh, heck, it's only a snail."

"Exactly—these guys are eating the marigolds. Let's look at your mom's Hostas. More! Pick 'em off and put 'em in the bag."

"It's sticky and slippery. He pulled back into his shell. Ha, he thinks he's hiding."

⭐12

"See that flat, squishy part? It's called the foot. That's how it glurps and glides along. Some people cook snails and eat them with butter and garlic."

"No way! Not me."

Gina laughed. "Let's keep them zipped tight in the bag. Later we'll show some to your mom and dad."

"Cool. Mom won't believe we did this. And tomato hornworms, too."

"We'll go snail hunting again tomorrow, Gai, because they go away and hide before sunrise and then come back at night. Now off to bed with you."

"Gina, I wanna free the fireflies first. Then they'll come back tomorrow night, too."

Next morning, Gina asked, "Does your mom ever use sprays in her garden?"

"Nah, nothing, ever. She says that stuff'd kill butterflies."

"Okay, great news!" She convinced Gai to bring along the bag of snails when they walked to the park. "Now that we know the snails are chemical-free, we're going to recycle them."

"Huh? Recycle snails? I thought we were gonna show them to Mom and Dad."

"We have two weeks to collect more. See those geese and ducks over there by the lake? Let's walk over very slowly. They'll think we're gonna feed them."

"But we didn't bring any bread."

"Nope, you're right. But we brought one of their favorite foods instead—snails!"

"Oh man, they're gobbling them up, shells and all! Now I know where to bring the snails when I catch 'em."

After lunch, the two spent more time in the garden.

"Gai, see those flowers where the butterflies are standing—the daisies, black-eyed Susans, and coneflowers?"

"Hey, the flowers are like landing pads for the butterflies, aren't they? Awesome."

"Exactly. That's so they can get nectar with their proboscis, Gai."

"Proboscis? Pro – bos – KISS? Kiss? Yuck!"

"It unfurls like an elephant's trunk to reach in and get the nectar."

"These flowers are called perennials, Gai. They bloom for a long time in the summer, die off, and go away with the frost. Then in the late spring when it warms up, they come back again."

"Sweet. We have a Go-Away-Come-Back garden," laughed Gai. "How do you know all this stuff?

"I took a couple classes at the college. You're right about going away and coming back. The flowers and fireflies do, the snails do, and even the butterflies and hummingbirds do."

"Hmmm . . . Mom and Dad, too, huh? And when you leave in a couple weeks, will you come back? Huh?" Gai asked.

"You betcha, buddy."

Gai and Gina spent time in the garden, snagging snails and hornworms, swimming in the park pool, and playing board and card games on showery days. Two weeks later, Mr. and Mrs. Andrews returned home.

"Hi, Gai-boy, we missed you," exclaimed Mrs. Andrews, giving him a big hug and kiss that he wiped off with his sleeve.

"Hi, Gina, you guys have a good time?" asked Mr. Andrews, as he hugged Gai and swung him in a circle.

"What's that?" asked Mrs. Andrews, pointing at the bag.

"Oh, Mom, wait'll you see," Gai said, thrusting the bag of stinky something at her. "We picked these from your garden. I named it the Go-Away-Come-Back Garden 'cause that's what all the flowers, snails, butterflies, and fireflies do—go away and then come back."

"Exactly right, son," said his dad.

"Thank you sooo much for catching these critters," said Mrs. Andrews. "Our garden looks beautiful."

"Gina, don't forget," said Gai, "you said you'd come back again, too."

"I'll come back," said Gina, getting into her car. "Promise!"

Go-Away-Come-Back Glossary

Camouflage .... A disguise, something that conceals and makes a thing look like something else. Butterflies and bugs have body markings that help them hide from their predators.

Clues .... Evidence, information, or details that show something. Clues help solve crimes, mysteries, or crossword puzzles.

Detective .... Someone who investigates and uses clues to solve a mystery.

Foliage .... Plant leaves.

Foot .... Not your foot, the snail's foot. It's the bottom muscle that the snail uses to move. Slime comes from the foot and helps the snail slither more easily.

Hosta .... A perennial plant that has pretty foliage and flowers that bloom in the summer. Deer, rabbits, and snails like this plant.

Lightning bugs .... Also called fireflies. An insect, a flying beetle whose body glows or lights up in the dark.

Magnifying glass .... Also called a hand lens and usually has a handle. It makes things appear larger than they are. Shows the details of an object.

Marigold .... A popular orange, red, or gold garden flower. It has a strong smell that some people and insects do not like. Snails and slugs find them delicious. An annual, not a perennial.

Nectar .... The sweet liquid in a flower. Bees, humming-birds, and butterflies love it. Nectar is the main ingredient in honey.

Proboscis .... The long snout or feeding tube on a butterfly that unfurls and sucks up nectar.

Perennial .... A plant that lives more than two years, especially a flowering plant that blooms over spring and summer, dies off in the winter, and returns the following spring.

Predator .... An enemy that hunts, kills and eats another.

Slimy .... Slippery, feels wet and sticky.

Snail .... Brown land snail with a shell; active in the garden at night or cloudy days and chews on the foliage of some flowers and foliage. A very common pest. Handpicking at night is one way to control snails.

Tomato hornworm .. A very large caterpillar that likes to feed on tomato plants. Their green color is camouflage and makes them blend in with the leaves and difficult to see.

About the Author

Sandy Baker is passionate about writing and gardening and thus combines the two in her gardening books for children. When she was about Gai's age, she and her scientific sleuth friend Teddy used to catch lightning bugs, snakes, Japanese beetles, and snails. To them, only the beetles were "bad guys" because they ate all the hollyhocks. Now after 15 years as a Sonoma County (CA) Master Gardener, Sandy knows a lot more about which critters are beneficial to our gardens. She is an advocate of kids getting outside to garden, whether it's for food or for fun! She also says, "Read, because readers are leaders!" Sandy loves to bicycle, take pictures, and travel with her husband. You can find out a lot more about Sandy and gardening on her website www.sandybakerwriter.com.

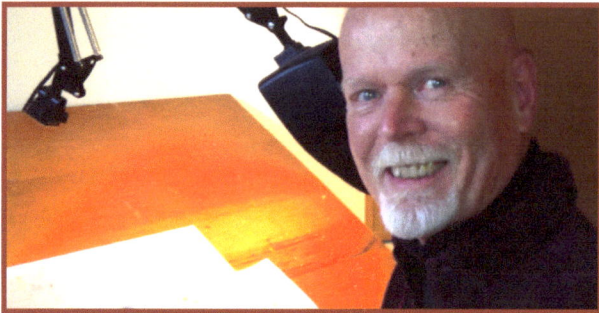

About the Illustrator

As a boy, Jack Wiens dreamed of working for Walt Disney and taught himself how to draw Mickey, Pluto and the gang. Although his primary career for 35 years was as a psychotherapist, he always kept creating art. Now a full-time illustrator, living in beautiful Ashland, Oregon, Jack is enjoying a new adventure. He teaches an art class at the local art center. He says, "I love seeing people find the joy of creating art. It's almost as fun as creating it myself!" Jack is father to a son and daughter and grandfather to three. He has had lots of fun drawing and painting with all of them over the years. You can view more of his work at www.jackwiens.com.

Acknowledgements

I continue to be ever-impressed and grateful for the book designs Rita Ter Sarkissoff has done for me. She is gifted, and each book she designs has been a gift to me and to our young readers. Thank you, Rita. I fell in love with Jack Wiens' illustrations of Gai. Jack beautifully captured Gai with his varied expressions of anger, joy, wonder, and happiness. After fifteen years as a Sonoma County Master Gardener, I still appreciate the program with its invaluable gardening information and member camaraderie.

www.ingramcontent.com/pod-product-compliance
Lightning Source LLC
Chambersburg PA
CBHW041552040426
42447CB00002B/161